Checkmate

The Black Schoolboy Who Beat a Chess Grandmaster at 12

Checkmate
The Black Schoolboy Who Beat a Chess Grandmaster at 12

BRIAN LEWIS

StoryTerrace

Text Simon Brooke, on behalf of StoryTerrace

Design StoryTerrace and Jelena Žarko

Copyright © Brian Lewis

Text is private and confidential

First print September 2021

StoryTerrace

www.StoryTerrace.com

CONTENTS

PROLOGUE

As I walked into the room, people were milling around and there was a buzz of chat. It was June and already it was becoming warm and stuffy. A few people turned to look at me. Some surprised, others clearly realising who I was, and looking at me with intense curiosity – and in some cases subtle disdain. Within moments I realised that I was the youngest person there by a long way. In the middle of the room a group of tables had been arranged in a large square. Spread across them were 20 chessboards, one for each player. The sight of the boards was, on the one hand comforting and familiar, but, on the other, it was terrifying.

This was it.

At the age of just 12 I was about to play chess against Michael Stean, an international grandmaster. The incredible journey that I had been on over the previous four years was coming to its climax. I'd studied Stean's classic moves and read up on his strategies and his overall approach to chess. I'd discussed my moves and my strategies with Mr Green, my chess teacher, and with other members of the chess club. But I knew that the chances of beating one of the greatest names in chess were incredibly low.

After a few moments we were invited to take our seats. I quickly sat down in the chair nearest me. My heart was beating hard in my chest and my palms felt sweaty and yet… I also felt quietly determined. I knew what I had to do, and I knew how to do it.

The games began. We players made our first moves and then Stean went from table to table responding, making it seem effortless and natural. As the process continued and more pieces came out from their first positions, with some being taken, he began to take a little more time over each board. Around us fans and supporters looked on, gripped by the tension. I could just hear a whispered commentary from around me, with the occasional intake of breath as a piece fell or Stean made a move that no one was expecting.

Stean continued to drift from one board to another, occasionally stroking his chin and frowning, and paying more attention to some boards than others. The idea that the grandmaster was having to study the board and consider his possible moves, rather than simply shift a piece from one square to another and step aside, was thrilling to us amateurs.

And then the first player lost to the grandmaster. There was a slight dip in the tension. It had finally happened. Someone had succumbed. A round of gentle applause and a shuffling as the defeated player stood up and left the table. Who would be next? Looking back, I realise that I was concentrating so hard on the board in front of me that I hardly noticed more people losing and then quietly leaving. I was completely focused on planning out my next moves and guessing what Stean would do next, based on my now detailed knowledge of his favourite strategies.

When I looked up after I don't know how long, the sun had moved away from the windows and the room seemed darker, more sombre. I realised that many of the other players had also been beaten and had gone. Stean was spending more and more time at each of the remaining players' boards – including mine.

Suddenly it was just Stean and me. There was a buzz around the room as he squared up to me and looked down at the board. The spectators had now gathered around us. I kept telling myself to hold my nerve. I just had to make sure that I focused and I didn't do anything silly. Stean was breathing deeply and frowning. He reached down and moved a piece.

Moments later he resigned. It took us all, I think, a moment just to take on board what had happened. We all peered at the board just to make sure. A moment later, Stean was holding out his hand. In a daze I took it. Mine seemed very small in comparison, and we shook.

"Well done, young man," he was saying.

"Thank you, Mr Stean," I said. "Thank you."

He smiled in a kindly way. He looked genuinely pleased for me. Then I became aware of a noise around us and I realised that the whole room was full of applause. The grown-ups around me looked thrilled, delighted and, in some cases, slightly mystified. Had this young black kid from a council estate really done it, really beaten a grandmaster?

The fact that I had actually won was beginning to sink in, and a wave of pride and pleasure washed over me. I couldn't wait to tell my mum and dad. But to be honest, I was only thinking about one person and what his reaction would be.

That person was Mr Green, my chess teacher. The man who'd sent me off on this remarkable journey and made this incredible victory possible.

The Bourne End Chess Club presented me with this Bobby Fischer book following my victory over Grandmaster Michael Stean

1

WELCOME TO BRITAIN

In 1963, an advertisement appeared in newspapers on the Caribbean island of Saint Vincent and my parents answered it. It was to change their lives – and it meant that my life has been very different from theirs. The advert invited people from Saint Vincent to emigrate to the UK. In particular, my mum and dad, who were newly married, were offered a new life in High Wycombe in Buckinghamshire.

Britain needed immigrants to work in the NHS, to drive buses, sit on production lines and to do many of the jobs that British people didn't want to do. My mum soon got a job as a nurse and my dad found work in a sweet factory. They were pleased to do it. The money was good and they honestly believed that Britain offered them and the children they were planning more opportunities than they'd find in Saint Vincent, beautiful though it was.

When I was 13, I visited the village that Mum and Dad had come from and that was a real eye-opener. The villagers shared a single standpipe for water and many of the houses were just made of what looked like hardboard. The streets were filled with deep potholes that the motorists zig-zagged around with amazing skill, while the educational and medical facilities were very basic. I remember standing there and thinking how lucky I was that my parents had made the tough decision to leave and come to the UK. I was also struck by how brave they must have been to leave their family and friends and to travel thousands of miles to somewhere they knew little about.

Saint Vincent and High Wycombe have a continuing relationship, but when Mr and Mrs Lewis arrived at their new home on a housing estate near the town of Micklefield, it wasn't just the weather that was cold and uninviting.

It was still possible to see signs on hostels and boarding houses in the big cities saying "no coloureds" and "no West Indians". Was there much evidence of that in Micklefield? I don't know, but my mum and dad were just one of 10 black families among hundreds of white households on this vast, sprawling estate. No wonder people stared at them. They must have seemed exotic but unnerving.

I was born in 1966 and my brother Raymond arrived in 1968. My parents had already realised that, as some of the very few black people living in the area, they had to keep themselves to themselves. It wasn't even easy to talk to your neighbours or the people behind the counters at the local shops. I realise now that many people on the estate thought that being West Indians, we'd be playing loud music and dealing drugs. I think they were actually slightly scared of us.

It was very difficult and sometimes quite frightening for my family. From a very young age we got used to name-calling, and one of my earliest memories is how, when we went off to school in the morning, we black kids from the estate would all walk together. I thought it was just somehow convenient, but it was only as I got a bit older that I realised that it was to try and ensure that we were OK, that we got to school safely.

Once we arrived at school, of course, we'd hear jokes about chocolate and monkeys from other kids. They just learnt it from their parents, I suppose, and they thought of it as just banter. We learnt to deal with it and got on with our lives. But even then, we black kids sat together in class and you knew that even if you started getting on with a white boy, there was no way you could go to his house for tea or anything like that. On Guy Fawkes Night, we had to watch the other people's fireworks from our garden because we would never be invited to someone's house for a party, and we knew that we wouldn't feel welcome at a public display.

Our life at home was a rich mix of British and Caribbean cultures. We watched British television and ate the food that my mum bought from the local supermarket. But I think my parents were keen to hang onto their traditions. We supported the West Indies cricket team and went wild when they won. We had to use coconut cream to moisturise our skin because of the dry, chilly British air, and my mum really struggled to find a barber who could cut our hair. No one around us had any experience of cutting black people's hair.

Our staple diet was rice and peas and chicken with plantain. Whenever we had Corn Flakes my mum would always heat up the milk. It was one of those quirky little things that I always remember. I think it was because it was so cold out of the fridge, and the fact that everything seemed so cold in England.

When I was about 10, we went on a school trip to the Isle of Wight. I was already a bit homesick I think, and ice-cold milk on my Corn Flakes just set me off. I remember crying when I saw the bowl in front of me, but one of the teachers was so touched that he had the cook heat the milk up for me. I think it was one of those little things that reminded me that I was different from 95% of the boys at school.

It was difficult to make friends at school outside the group of other black kids. When we played football, we'd divide into the white team and the black team. I don't think that anyone was being consciously racist – it was just a natural dividing line and so that's how it worked out. The problem was that because there were so many more white kids, their team would usually be twice as big as ours. It certainly trained us to do our best and play hard.

Sometimes if a white boy went too far in the playground with the banter, we'd fight back. We'd be scrapping on the ground with them until a teacher came and broke it up. You could hardly blame us, but unfortunately it fed into that stereotype of West Indians being aggressive. Most of the teachers wanted to support us and help us to fit in, but they found it difficult to relate to us, I think. Almost none had had any direct experience of black boys and they knew very little about our culture. They knew how to stop someone being bullied if they were fat or shy, but when it came to skin colour, well that was something else. There was no training in race relations that I ever heard of, but the teachers just did their best to be fair – with a few exceptions.

Eventually, though, the white kids started mingling with the black kids and we began to realise from our own experience that, actually, we really weren't that different from each other. We all liked playing cricket and football and watching *Doctor Who* and eating ice cream on the way home during the summer term. I remember that after a few years, my mum became good friends with our next-door neighbour. Because of the lack of race relations back then, it was just a slow and difficult education process for all of us.

The thing that helped me in particular was that it soon became clear that I was pretty bright. Even then I think some of the teachers couldn't quite believe it – despite the stereotypes, a young black kid was good at maths. I don't know why – I just enjoyed it. I think I liked the methodology and the patterns, and I found that I could learn the algorithms and the equations.

My mum and dad didn't get involved with our schoolwork,

but they always pushed us to work hard and do well. Even though my dad worked long hours in the sweet factory making Crunchie bars among other things, and did various other jobs including working as a welder, while my mum covered five nights a week at the general hospital, from 8 p.m. to 8 a.m, they made sure that my brother, Raymond, and I did our homework and always got to school on time.

My mum and dad were kind and loving to us, but they were serious, hard-working people. Ensuring that there was food on the table and enough 50 pence pieces for the electricity meter was a constant battle. For them, difficult and even hostile though it could be, Britain was a land of opportunity, and they were determined that their sons would make the most of all it offered and do better than them in their careers.

But they could never have anticipated a particular opportunity that would come my way thanks to a remarkable teacher.

History of Chess

It's thought that people have been playing chess for nearly 15 centuries. An early version of the game probably started in India in the seventh century before moving through Persia (modern-day Iran) and the Byzantine Empire and then via various Muslim trade routes into north Africa and southern Europe. The game also spread into Russia thanks to Slav traders. It reached as far as Iceland courtesy of the Vikings, who are thought to be responsible for 78 pieces carved from walrus ivory that were found on the Isle of Lewis in the Outer Hebrides in 1831 and probably date from the 11th or 12th century. During the Middle Ages, the game was favoured by kings and rulers, which boosted its image. Rule changes over the centuries have seen "the counsellor" become "the queen" and gain much greater ability to move around the board.

The first championship of modern times took place in 1834, when the Frenchman Louis-Charles de la Bourdonnais of Paris beat his opponent, Londoner, Alexander McDonnell. Official tournaments followed in London, New York and across Europe over subsequent years as the appeal of the game increased. In Paris in 1924, representatives of 15 countries met to organise the first permanent international chess federation, the Fédération Internationale des Échecs (FIDE), *échecs* being French for chess. By the mid-1990s around 2,000 FIDE tournaments were taking place every year, more than 50 times the number that had done so during the 1950s.

As a child playing chess in Micklefield County Combined School, I had no idea what a great tradition I was following in. Even if I had known, I probably wouldn't have cared. I just loved the game.

Born to be chess champions

The chess champion!

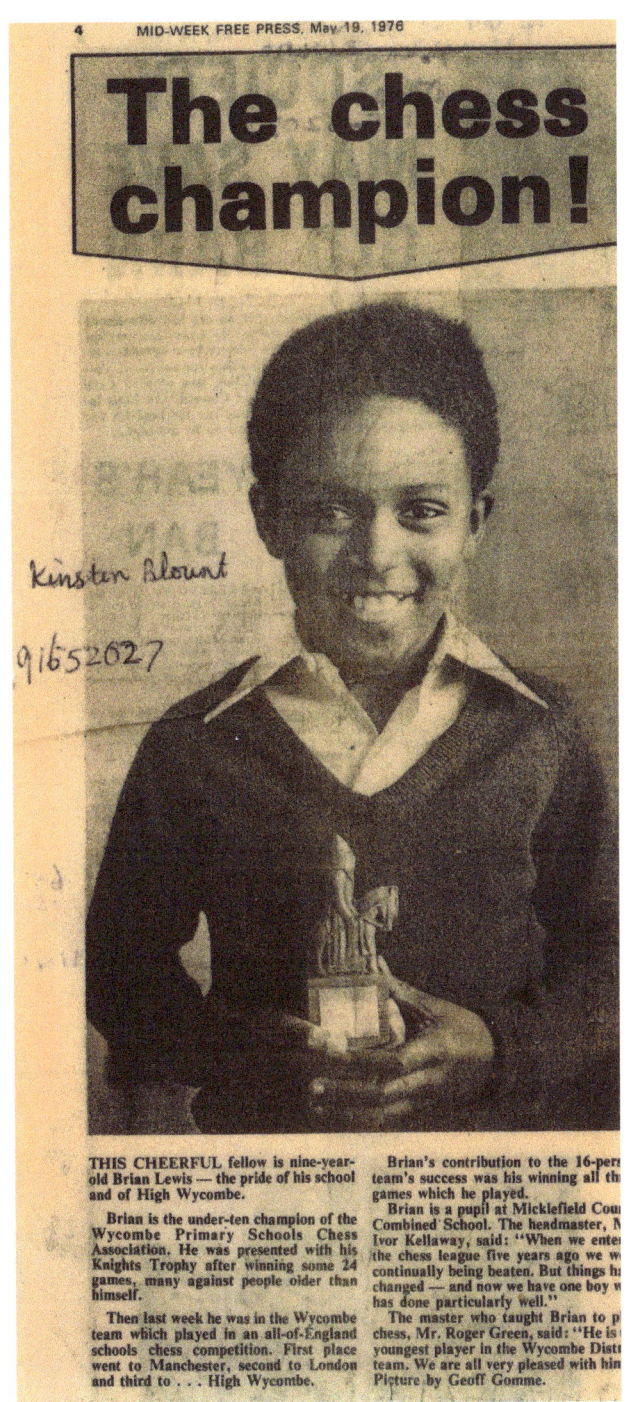

Kinsten Blount

91652027

THIS CHEERFUL fellow is nine-year-old Brian Lewis — the pride of his school and of High Wycombe.

Brian is the under-ten champion of the Wycombe Primary Schools Chess Association. He was presented with his Knights Trophy after winning some 24 games, many against people older than himself.

Then last week he was in the Wycombe team which played in an all-of-England schools chess competition. First place went to Manchester, second to London and third to . . . High Wycombe.

Brian's contribution to the 16-per[son] team's success was his winning all th[e] games which he played.

Brian is a pupil at Micklefield Cou[nty] Combined School. The headmaster, M[r] Ivor Kellaway, said: "When we enter[ed] the chess league five years ago we w[ere] continually being beaten. But things h[ave] changed — and now we have one boy w[ho] has done particularly well."

The master who taught Brian to p[lay] chess, Mr. Roger Green, said: "He is [the] youngest player in the Wycombe Distr[ict] team. We are all very pleased with him[."] Picture by Geoff Gomme.

The Chess Champion! This cheerful fellow is the nine-year-old Brian Lewis – the pride of his school and of High Wycombe

2

ENTER MR GREEN

When Mr Green walked into the classroom one warm, sunny Monday morning at the start of the autumn term, even as an eight-year-old I knew he was different from most of the other teachers. He was tall and gangly. He had long, crazy hair like a popstar and he wore trendy wide collars and bell-bottom trousers. Looking back, I'm sure the older teachers didn't approve of him. And it wasn't just his clothes. Unlike most of his colleagues, he seemed to want to get to know us as people, to understand us.

He spent time talking to us and listening to us, and his whole attitude to school and teaching was unlike anything we'd experienced so far. I think he was more tuned into race issues, too. He clearly had a vocation, and you just got the feeling that he cared. He'd sit on the floor with us and walk across the grass with us when junior boys weren't supposed to. He'd ask us about our home lives, what we enjoyed doing outside school, what we watched on telly, and he made learning fun. Most of all, though, he seemed just very, very cool.

One day he came into the classroom and, instead of asking us about our maths or English homework, he told us that he had started a chess club a couple of years earlier and he wanted us to join. We were all around eight years old and I don't think most of the class even knew what chess was, so the idea that boys from a school like Micklefield would develop an interest in chess seemed incredible. The village school down the road probably played it, but not us – especially not black kids. If we'd known what the word "sceptical" meant, then that's how we'd have described our reaction. There was also the simple fact that we were boys – we wanted to play cricket and football and run around, not sit at desks, staring at boards covered with weird looking little objects. Raymond and I occasionally played draughts at home, but that was only when there was nothing else to do. Had we got this new teacher wrong? Was he not so cool, after all?

It wasn't just we boys who weren't keen. Looking back, there was clearly some resentment from the other teachers and a few of the parents about the amount of time and resources that this chess thing was taking up. Was it really worth it? some people wondered. What was the point?

But Mr Green wasn't going to give up on his idea of teaching us chess so easily. He'd already founded a chess club at what was then a care home for orphaned kids next to the school. I remember there was one boy who played chess there, and we began to play with him too. He was mixed race. Back then, if a woman had a child with a black man the stigma was so bad that she'd often give the child away.

Barry George was a black child who had grown up in the care system and he joined the chess club with Raymond and me. He was an exciting player with great flair. He would study the game a length and he was known for his ruthless, attacking style. His enthusiasm and his energy really helped to raise the game of all of his fellow chess club members.

There was another kid who was bigger than the rest of the kids his age and he looked older and so somehow didn't fit in with everyone else, but Mr Green encouraged him to play and he loved it. I think that it was a way that this kid could feel one of the gang, just like everyone else. And that was so important – looking back, I realise that chess offered a way for any kid, whatever their colour, whatever their background, to interact with other kids and to be accepted. I think that he might also have seen it as a way of encouraging black and white kids to get together in an informal environment.

Mr Green could have taught at any school, and it would have been much easier for him to establish a chess club at a village school or a private school, but I think he genuinely believed that chess had something to offer kids from less well-off homes who went to a comprehensive. He realised that chess didn't have to be something that was only available to kids from a better-off background, that youngsters like us could also enjoy it and benefit from playing it. The assumption among many teachers was, I think, that boys like us would only want to do physical things such as play football and cricket in our spare time, rather than doing something that used our brains, but Mr Green saw it another way.

He'd been playing since he was our age, he told us, and the more he talked about this game, with all its strategies and complications and, to be honest, the ruthless competition that it involved, the more his enthusiasm began to infect us.

Finally, we agreed to start playing. So, instead of rushing outside to kick a ball around one particular lunch break, a small group of us gathered around a board as Mr Green began to explain to us how each piece could move across it. At first, we thought we'd never remember what a knight could do and where we could move a queen. But when we divided up into twos and started moving them around, performing the simple opening moves that Mr Green had taught us, it slowly began to make sense. I think, being boys, we liked the element of competition. We were actually looking forward to doing it again the following week.

When the chess club first started, we'd meet together for about an hour or so after school. It shows how keen we were to play this intriguing game and how contagious Mr Green's enthusiasm was that we were willing to stay behind instead of getting off home the way almost all the other boys were.

I think we were already beginning to get hooked by this stage. Mr Green produced some chessboards and we began to play games between us. I don't know where he got those boards from. Perhaps he bought them himself, because I don't think the school had ever had a supply of chessboards. After all, we were the first to play it at Micklefield.

Learning the moves and the basic strategies was a slow process because there was only Mr Green to teach us. He would walk around between the desks, asking how we were getting on, reminding us how the pieces could move when we forgot, and encouraging us to start thinking about our strategies. We didn't really know what we were doing, but he was so patient, taking us through it stage by stage. Sometimes some of us would get disillusioned because we couldn't remember every move, or we just seemed to keep losing game after game. But Mr Green was great at encouraging us and persuading us to come back the following week to have another go. We began to meet more often, getting together twice a week at lunchtime as well as for the after-school sessions.

It's worth remembering that at this time, in the mid-1970s, there were no computers in schools and homes and certainly no internet. You couldn't just go online to learn about new chess moves or to study how the grandmasters developed their strategies. Everything we learnt came from Mr Green and a few books that he brought in to the Chess Club for us to share.

I remember coming home following the first meeting of the chess club and being so excited about what I'd learnt. I told my mum and dad, and even though they were a bit surprised – they didn't know much about chess and they'd certainly never believed that I might be interested in it, I don't think – they seemed pleased for me. When I look back, I think what they really liked was the idea that playing this game was a way of us integrating more, of us mixing with the white kids and being accepted. I realised pretty early on that, unlike other aspects of my life, especially school, with the chess club the fact that I was black and part of a small minority didn't matter.

During break times, while we were having lunch or when we walked home from school, we'd tend to gravitate towards the other black kids, while the white kids hung around with the other kids who were white. The black boys might not speak to the white boys, but then we'd all mix together at the chess club without even thinking about it. There was very little focus on developing good race relations at the school, because back in the 1970s few people thought that it was particularly important and rarely worked towards integrating the races and creating some kind of racial harmony.

But we all mixed together in the chess club, black kids and white. During those lunch breaks and sessions after school, as we gathered around our chessboards and began to focus on the game, race was never an issue. And that's the thing about a game like chess – when you sit down at the board to play someone, the colour of your skin, your social class or where you come from doesn't matter. Even your age isn't that important. You can be a kid who's been playing for just a few years and you can still beat a pro who's had decades of experience – as I know.

Why did I take so readily to chess? At the time I never questioned it. I just loved playing. Thinking about it, though, it was probably connected with the fact that I discovered that I was good at maths. I liked the logic, the way the pieces each had their own rules and limitations, the idea that if you move this piece here, then the logical consequences will be this. I began to realise that I could identify patterns on the board that lots of other players couldn't. I could see that if I went here, my opponent would go there, and this would happen at the other end of the board and that would be the most likely result.

Yes, and I was a boy, of course, so I was competitive. It was the same when I played football and cricket. I liked taking someone on and beating them. But we'd always shake hands afterwards. That was another thing about Mr Green's chess club – competition soon became fierce and we were all determined to win, but we never fell out. It was always good natured. And that was something that Mr Green drummed into us right from the start. We had to do our best to beat our opponent, but what really counted was good sportsmanship. It's a lesson that I've never forgotten.

Chess on Screen, Stage and in Print

The Queen's Gambit was an unexpected hit when it aired on Netflix, making it the channel's most-watched scripted miniseries, and its top show in 63 countries. Beth Harmon is an orphan – and a chess prodigy. The story starts in the mid-1950s and we watch as Harmon, played by Anya Taylor-Joy – who has won a number of awards, including the Golden Globe for best actress in a limited series, anthology series or a motion picture made for television – fights her way to the top of the chess world while struggling with drug and alcohol dependency. A classic tale of triumph over adversity, the series, which is based on a book, gets its title from one of the oldest known moves in chess, dating back to the 15th century.

However, *The Queen's Gambit* is only one of a number of films, plays and books that have featured chess. The Cold War provides the backdrop for *Chess*, a musical with music by Benny Andersson and Björn Ulvaeus of the pop group ABBA, based on a book by lyricist Tim Rice. Although the characters are fictional, it's often been suggested that the grandmaster in the story is based on Bobby Fischer, who at the age of just 14 became the youngest ever US Chess Champion. The tale was inspired, it's thought, by the careers of Russian grandmasters Viktor Korchnoi and Anatoly Karpov.

The highly praised film *Searching for Bobby Fischer* is not actually about Fischer, but it concerns another young prodigy who plays chess with fans of the game in Washington Square Park, New York. His mentor is a black chess hustler called Vinnie, played by Laurence Fishburne, who adopts an in-your-face approach to the game, complete with unorthodox strategies.

In *Chess Story* by Stefan Zweig, the mysterious Dr B, a chess obsessive who's recovering from a nervous breakdown, is travelling on an ocean liner from New York to Buenos Aires during the Second World War. Also on board is a group of chess players who keep losing to their fellow passenger, World Chess Champion Mirko Czentovic. It's only when Dr B steps in to help them out that Czentovic comes under pressure in this eerie thriller.

Why does chess work so well in fiction? Well, I think it's because at its heart it has confrontation, tension and complex strategies – all of which are essential ingredients for a great story.

Mr Green and his chess team

3

OUR FIRST PROPER MATCH

"Good news, boys," said Mr Green as we started our lunchtime chess group one day. "I've managed to arrange a match with another school."

We were all nervous about our first tournament, but mainly very excited. After lessons we piled into the school bus and set off. We began to get more anxious, though, as we approached the school. It was set back from the road, it was an elegant, ancient-looking building, surrounded by rolling green playing fields and the boys wore smart blazers and colourful ties. We suddenly became very conscious that this place was posh – very posh. Mr Green sensed our anxiety, I think, and he began to crack jokes and give us a little pep talk.

We were led along corridors past classrooms that didn't look anything like ours, with teachers and boys who didn't look anything like us. Finally, we arrived at what seemed to be a great hall. The boards were laid out on tables and

I think we all felt slightly more relaxed seeing something so familiar. After all, chess was what we were there for. But there were bottles of orange squash, crisps, sandwiches and a whole table full of other goodies – this school was clearly in a different league to ours. The teachers gave us a warm welcome and invited us to dig in. The boys seemed tall and confident, and somehow even more intimidating.

After some small talk we were invited to sit down and start playing. I caught my friends' eyes and some of us whispered "good luck" to each other. I opened with one of my favourite moves and prepared for what I thought my opponent would do in return. But he didn't. He moved his pieces in a way that I wasn't expecting. I was completely confused. This wasn't what I'd anticipated at all. This boy was playing at a completely different level. I didn't know what he was going to do next. After about an hour it was checkmate. He was very nice and offered to shake my hand, but I was just so surprised and I felt embarrassed. As we stopped for a break with more orange squash, sandwiches and crisps, I realised that I wasn't the only one. My mates were also losing around me. Their faces were grim and angry. Mr Green gave us a pep talk and reminded us that it wasn't over yet.

But then, after another hour or so, it was over. And we'd lost. Every single one of us had been defeated in our individual games against the posh boys. We'd lost our first tournament badly. We'd crashed and burned.

This wasn't supposed to happen. We were Micklefield.

We were good, really good. Weren't we? I think we all sort of realised that these boys weren't just better than us, they were playing a different type of game. It was more subtle, more considered. It seemed to involve more strategies. These boys were adopting a more long-term view and not rushing to take our pieces. Suddenly, we were finding that we were stuck – it was checkmate.

I realised that my approach to chess like my approach to draughts. My dad had taught Raymond, my brother, and me to attack as soon as we could and to overwhelm the opposition. I think there was something deeper here, something more than what was happening on the chessboard. He'd decided that, as a young black man, I'd have to be tough and be ready to go on the offensive to defend myself. It was well meant, but it wasn't right for this new, high-level chess that we were playing.

The mood on the bus going back was awful. It was getting dark by then and Mr Green drove us back in silence. Some of the boys were fighting back tears, staring out of the windows so that they couldn't be seen to be crying. It was miserable. We just felt so humiliated. How were we going to tell our parents? How were we going to face the other kids at school? Many of us were just wondering whether chess really was for us. Perhaps it was a game that was only for the posh boys we'd met that evening, not for boys from a council estate.

Looking back, I think that perhaps Mr Green deliberately

threw us in at the deep end. He knew that it would be tough for us – although I don't think he reckoned we'd be trounced quite as badly as that – but he believed that it would a useful learning experience. We'd understand that these boys were playing a different kind of game – but it was one that we could master if we stuck at it. We'd also understand how to lose gracefully – and we had, despite our utter despondency. More importantly, I think Mr Green wanted us to understand that with chess, every time you lose a match you learn something new.

"Treat defeat as a learning experience," he told us, even though we weren't yet in the mood to think about it like that. "Look at what your opponent did and learn from it. That's a good lesson for life."

The first meeting of the chess club after this crashing defeat was pretty awful. We trudged into the classroom and, for the first time, none of us really felt like playing.

But Mr Green was great at rallying us again. He persuaded the members who wanted to give up that they should stick with it, and he began to explain to us why we'd lost and what these boys knew that we didn't. We'd only been defeated, he pointed out, because we hadn't been prepared for these particular chess moves. Once we recognised them and knew how to neutralise them, we'd have nothing to fear. Most of us still weren't sure. We'd had a real beating, after all. But that was the thing about Mr Green – his enthusiasm was infectious.

"Don't worry, guys, you can learn these moves, these strategies too," he told us. "It's just a case of knowing them and being ready to put them into practice. OK, let's get to work. I'll show you."

And we did. We gathered around the board and he demonstrated the new moves to us. The four-move checkmate, which many of our opponents had used so successfully against us, he explained, is actually very common. He took us through it. Suddenly, it all became clear. Yes, it was devastating – but only if you didn't know what you were doing. Now we did. The atmosphere in the room was transformed. Suddenly, we couldn't wait to try out the four-move checkmate and the other new moves that he'd shown us.

One of these was the Ruy Lopez. Sometimes known as the Spanish Opening or the Spanish Move, it's named after a sixteenth century Spanish priest. It's effective but it's also a great move for relative beginners as I was then, because it leads to an open game with the potential for lots of further moves for both players. I practiced it again and again, first with Mr Green and then with my fellow chess club members. We all felt so much more confident with these extra moves an openings in our tool box.

We were up for it. Once again, Micklefield were back in the game. And we were out to win.

Ten Fascinating Facts About Chess

1. "Checkmate," it's thought, comes from the Persian phrase *shah mat*, meaning "the King is dead".

2. According to Trekkie chess fans, Kirk and Spock have played chess three times on *Star Trek*. Kirk has won all three games.

3. A "Knight's tour" features over 122 million possibilities.

4. A computer program named Deep Thought beat an international grandmaster for the first time in November 1988, in Long Beach, California.

5. The worst recorded performance by a chess player was Nicholas Macleod of Canada, who lost 31 games in the New York double round-robin of 1889, finishing last out of 20 players.

6. The longest chess game, in theory anyway, possible involves 5,949 moves.

7. Approximately 600 million people are thought to be able to play chess worldwide.

8. Emanuel Lasker, a German doctor, held the title of World Chess Champion for about 27 years, from 1894 to 1920, the longest reign of an officially recognised chess champion.

9. Chess was the first game to be played in space. In June 1970, the Soyuz 9 crew, Vitaly Sevastyanov and Andrian Nikolayev, played against their ground-control team. The game ended in a draw.

10. The youngest World Chess Champion was the Soviet player Garry Kasparov, who was just 22 years old when he won in 1985.

My first chess award presented by the headmaster Mr Kellogs

My first chess championship award

4

FIGHTING BACK

I won't say that we were confident as we set off a few months later to play another school, but at least we felt better prepared than we had been during our first tournament. We'd been bloodied. But least we now knew what to expect. As well as the four-move checkmate, Mr Green had taught us some other strategies and we'd practiced them among ourselves in our lunch breaks. We had raised our game and we knew it. We felt empowered, I think.

It wasn't just that we'd learnt new moves, though. We'd also learnt how to take the pressure, how to stay calm, how to anticipate our opponent's next move, how to take the longer, strategic view – and how to lose. As we approached another big, posh school in our school van, Mr Green carried on with his little pep talk, reminding us of what we'd learnt and encouraging us to stay calm, take our time and think through our strategies. We shouldn't feel rushed and we shouldn't feel intimidated.

"You've prepared and you've practised, and that's all you

can do," he told us, as he drove us through the imposing gates of the school. Looking back, I think he was probably talking to himself as much as he was talking to us.

Well, we lost again.

But this time it wasn't a walkover. We actually won one of the five games. Yep, we won. OK, it wasn't a triumph, but for us, coming from such a low base, with the memory of being trounced in our match still fresh in our minds, it was enough. We were absolutely ecstatic. We laughed, shouted and joked on the bus all the way back to Micklefield, and Mr Green, I reckon, as he drove us and laughed along with our jokes, was probably even more pleased and relieved than we were. After all, he'd taken a risk putting us up for another match – and it had paid off.

It was about then, during that autumn term, a year after the chess club had started, that I began to realise that I was the best player in our club. Every time I played a match, I seemed to be beating the other players. We had boards ranging from one to six, depending on people's ability and their victories, and by Christmas time I found myself being put on board one. Yes, we were very competitive, but it was good to see that the other members of the club were actually pleased for me. I think that's because we learned from each other.

At this point I couldn't even practise outside school, because I didn't have a chessboard at home. I was just playing during all the spare time I had at school. Mr Green did start saying to me: "Brian, you seem to have a talent for chess."

That was incredibly encouraging, and it just made me want to work harder than ever at it. I couldn't really get big-headed about the idea, though, because chess was really a minority sport – to put it mildly – at Micklefield. It wasn't like being good at football or cricket. Chess just wasn't on most boys' radars. My younger brother, Raymond, was probably the only other boy who was excited for me, but that didn't matter. My mum and dad still couldn't relate to this chess business, but I think they were becoming more interested and they were just pleased that their son was so good at something and was enjoying it so much. They also picked up, I think, on how it helped us to integrate better, and that was important to them.

I was also becoming increasingly aware of news reports about chess. The rivalry between the US and what was then the USSR was reported on the front pages of the newspapers, and even though I never really watched much of the news on television, whenever an item about chess matches between the Americans and the Soviets popped up, I'd follow it.

On 11th July 1972, just a few years before I'd started to play, Bobby Fischer, who had won the US Chess Championships eight times, faced the brilliant Russian player and reigning World Champion Boris Spassky in what has become known as the "Match of the Century". It was all the more tense – and politically significant – because, for the 24 years prior to this match, the Russians had held the World Championship title.

The Soviet Union saw its chess prowess as proof that its ideology was superior to that of the Americans. At the 1972 game, Fischer threatened to walk away, having lost the first game. However, US National Security Adviser Henry Kissinger called him and persuaded him to continue playing. In the end, after 21 games spread over two months, Fischer finally won. And so had the Americans, it was felt.

At Micklefield, as we played more games, we naturally improved. We were learning new strategies and were developing in confidence. I was beginning to realise just how complex and multidimensional chess is – and how many different ways there are to achieve that all important checkmate.

The rest of the school was certainly taking more notice of us by this time. In 1976, I lead the High Wycombe chess team to third place, behind Manchester and London, in the All of England Schools Chess Competition. Mr Green pointed out to us that Manchester had a population of around half a million potential chess players, while London had a whopping eight million or so. Both of them dwarfed High Wycombe's population of 100,000. It was a David and Goliath-style victory, we decided.

As we were preparing to shuffle out of the assembly hall on a sunny day in the middle of May, ready for our first lesson, the headmaster, Mr Kellaway, stopped us. He held up a newspaper cutting. I saw my beaming face in the photo and I immediately knew what it was. "I want to congratulate Brian Lewis," the headmaster's booming voice told the whole school, "on a fantastic win at a national chess tournament."

Then, as other boys turned to look at me, he read the article out loud: "This cheerful fellow is nine-year-old Brian Lewis – the pride of his school and of High Wycombe. Brian is the Under-10 Champion of the Wycombe Primary Schools Chess Association. He was presented with his Knights Trophy after winning some 24 games, many against people older than himself. Then last week he was in the Wycombe team that played in the All of England Schools Chess Competition. First place went to Manchester, second to London and third to… High Wycombe. Brian's contribution to the 16-person team's success was his winning all three games which he played. Brian is a pupil at Micklefield County Combined School. The headmaster, Mr Ivor Kellaway, said: 'When we entered the chess league five years ago, we were continually being beaten. But things have changed – and now we have one boy who has done particularly well.' The master who taught Brian to play chess, Mr Roger Green, said: 'He is the youngest player in the Wycombe District team. We are all very pleased with him.'

I love Mr Green's understated quote in the article. He was a modest man and didn't want to hog the limelight or get too emotional. My mum showed the newspaper clipping to her friends and neighbours and then saved it in her photo album.

Did it to anything to help the image of black people living in the area? I don't know, but I like to think that more people realised that we were every bit as intelligent and hard-working as white people, and perhaps it challenged some of the unhelpful stereotypes that were imposed on the Afro-Caribbean population back then.

The following year, 1977, saw us enter a tougher competition and we didn't do as well. Our team had worked hard learning new moves and perfecting our game, but so had the other players. Everyone said that it was a very strong year for chess. We were runners up that year, but it was still a remarkable achievement for a small town with none of the prestigious colleges and public schools that the big cities had. Already, High Wycombe – and Micklefield School in particular – was making a name for itself in the world of school chess.

Yes, we were disappointed as we set off home, following our success the previous year, but Mr Green buoyed us up again and, in comparison with our thrashing at that first match against the posh school down the road, it was just a little stumble.

However, the next year, 1978, we triumphed again as I became Under-11 Champion. That's not the only reason I remember that particular year. It was also the year when I beat Mr Green.

We'd played before and, naturally, he'd always won. But I think that time we both realised that something special was happening. And we weren't the only ones. After a while the whole chess club had finished their games and had gathered around the desk where we were playing. I was still thinking, though, yeah, at any minute, he's going to beat me. After all, he'd been playing for 10 or 15 years at least, and I'd only started four years ago. Surely, he'd pull something out of his hat and beat me?

But he didn't. He resigned. I'd won. I'd beaten Mr Green, the man who taught me chess in the first place. It was a long, drawn-out game with very few pieces left on the board, but finally I took his queen and he realised he had no options left. He stood up and shook hands and said, "Well done." He was a very quiet, modest man, but it was an emotional moment for both of us, for teacher and pupil. The fact that I could now beat the person who had trained and guided me was a major milestone. I think it made me realise that I could be even more ambitious with my game.

In 1979, my fellow chess-club member John Doyle battled through to become Under-12 Champion. I was so pleased for him – and yes, just a little bit jealous. But I was also aware that it was another victory for Mr Green and his untiring, selfless devotion to the chess club that he'd founded. I was so pleased when the following year, 1980, my younger brother Ray became Under-12 Champion. There was definitely a bit of sibling rivalry in this case, but again I was very pleased for him. I'd seen how hard he'd worked, and it was great to see that pay off for him – as well as seeing the look of pride on my mum and dad's faces.

Under Mr Green's leadership and thanks to his unfailing enthusiasm and encouragement, Micklefield went on to win the Under-12s All of England Schools Chess Competition in 1981 and 1982. In both those years, it was girls who became champions and, looking back, that was great to see.

But I was heading for a new milestone with my game.

Chess and the Human Brain

Learning and playing chess benefits the human brain in a number of ways, scientists are discovering. The game's complex rules and myriad moves can improve memory, and good players have been shown to have better-than-average memories.

Chess is particularly good for the mental development of adults and young people. The prefrontal cortex is the last part of the brain to develop during adolescence. It's responsible for skills such as rational thinking, self-control, judgement and planning. Given the importance in chess of strategic and critical thinking, it can help the development of the prefrontal cortex in young people.

A research project by the US Chess Federation took a group of 53 elementary school students in New York City and, over a number of years, used technology to measure the reading ability of those who played chess compared with those who didn't. The chess players displayed a noticeable improvement in their reading skills over those students who didn't play. More generally, a study of around 4,000 students from Venezuela showed that playing chess can significantly increase IQ scores after just four months of play.

With Alzheimer's on the increase, it's interesting to note a study reported in the *New England Journal of Medicine* that discovered that those over 75 years old who play games such as chess are less likely to develop dementia than their peers who don't.

Another benefit of chess that I've seen for myself is that it helps people to work together, regardless of their age, background or race – and, once they're playing, it encourages them to see past these superficial differences.

UNDER TEN Champion of Wycombe Primary Schools Chess Association, Brian Lewis (aged 9) at Micklefield County Combined School, is presented with his Knight Trophy by his headmaster, Mr Ivor Kellaway. Brian was in the Wycombe team which came third in the All-England schools chess tourney, winning all his games.

Local newspaper article – presentation from my school headmaster

BUCKS FREE PRESS, April 7, 1978

Chess champs line-up

Here are the three winners in the Micklefield School chess championship. From left to right they are: John Doyle first; Brian Lewis, second and Brian Smyth third.

Local press article

Bucks champion

5

BOURNE END CHESS CLUB

Mr Green had realised by this stage that I needed new challenges – and new opportunities. The Bourne End Chess Club was the most celebrated in Buckinghamshire and it's still very highly regarded in the world of chess. I'd already met some of the players from matches that I'd played, and I knew that they were at a particularly high standard.

Mr Green explained that they'd be willing to take me on. For a young black kid from a state school, this was pretty amazing, but it turned out that the chairman had read about my success and he wanted to have me on board. I was nervous, obviously, but also thrilled and really looking forward to meeting some great players and upping my game.

But then my hopes were dashed. It was such a silly thing, but I simply couldn't get there. My mum and dad were both working and the club was six or seven miles away from home. I couldn't walk there. As a young lad, it would have been too far and perhaps even too dangerous. It seemed like a disaster. My hopes had been raised, but then I was devastated.

But then the chairman made a generous offer. He was so keen to have me as a member of the club that he said would pick me up and take me back again. I remember being almost as excited about his cool, smart car as I was about actually going to the club itself.

Everyone at Bourne End was very friendly and welcoming – as well as being a little bit curious about this young black kid who was supposed to be such a prodigy. It was intimidating to be faced by so many adults, but I remembered the pep talks and the reassurance that Mr Green had given me. Yes, I was going to play grown-ups for the first time, but I can do this, I told myself, as I walked in and was introduced. I can beat these players too.

When I arrived, the chess club had a chart on the wall with a list of each player numbered from one to 50, with the best player listed at number one and the lowest ranked player at number 50 – this is called a chess rating system. A chess rating system is a system used in chess to estimate the strength of a player, based on their performance versus other players. It reminded me of a football league table and when I joined, I was at the bottom and the only way to climb up the ladder was to beat the player one or two places above you by challenging them. These league matches stipulated that you could only play a player one or two places above you and of course you play those below you as well. During a chess evening you would play those above and below you and the club will move you up or down the table at the end of the evening (a bit like snakes and ladders). The drive and focus was to get into the top 20 so that you can play in the first team as well as be invited to play grandmasters in simultaneous chess games. I soon climbed the table rapidly by beating most of the players I challenged, and it was fair to say that I created a buzz because this 11/12 year old who had only started playing chess for four years was beating seasoned adult players fairly convincingly. I recall the chairman dropping me home each evening and chatting about certain moves that I made, and it was only a few months before he had told me that I had made the first team who played against other chess clubs. I played a handful of first team games and won most of my matches before I was told that I had been selected to play the Grandmaster, Michael Stean, which was so exciting, and I couldn't sleep well for days before the match on the 3rd June 1978.

It was a Saturday and I remember going into school afterwards and I couldn't wait to find Mr Green to tell him. There were no mobile phones back then, so he simply didn't know what had happened. When I told him at the start of the first chess club that week, he broke into a huge smile and shook hands excitedly. He was just so pleased for me – as were the other players.

"Well done, Brian, well done, that's amazing," he kept saying. I think for him it was a vindication of all the risks that he had taken and all the effort that he had put it in to teaching us chess.

I loved my time at Bourne End, and my victory against Michael Stean there was the crowning achievement of my time as a chess champion.

After that, my circumstances changed in a way that made my commitment to chess much more difficult. My mum had my baby brother, Michael, when I was 13 years old, and she also split up from my dad at about that time. As a result, I had to take on the responsibility of looking after a baby while my mum went to work her night shifts at the hospital. I loved taking care of young Michael but it meant that, along with the other responsibilities that I now had to deal with, there was simply no time to sit down and play chess.

I left home at 22, but I didn't go to university. I wanted to do something more practical and get into the world of work as soon as I could. So, instead, I did business studies at the local college and became a qualified accountant some years later. They often say that chess players are good at maths, but my love of chess helped me in more ways than that. It taught me the importance of focusing on a task in hand, of learning new skills and of practising them. My experience with tournaments was a great way of understanding how to handle exam nerves, too.

I was still very young when I met Susan, the woman who was to become my wife. She is a lawyer and we now have three kids. My youngest child is now 15 and played chess for the county when he was 11. I was so proud of him – and I still am.

Micklefield Chess Champions – John Doyle and Brian Smyth

StoryTerrace